STYLIN' SHOW

Written by Christine Peymani

 **PaRragon**

Bath · New York · Singapore · Hong Kong · Cologne · Delhi · Melbourne

First published by Parragon in 2008
Parragon
Queen Street House
4 Queen Street
Bath BA1 1HE, UK

Copyright © 2008 TM & © MGA Entertainment, Inc.

All rights reserved. No part of this publication may be
reproduced, stored in a retrieval system or transmitted, in any
form or by any means, electronic, mechanical, photocopying,
recording or otherwise, without the prior permission of the
copyright holder.

ISBN 978-1-4075-2501-3

Printed in UK

CHAPTER 1

"And now, for our featured performers, the Soaring Santinis!" shouted the ringmaster, tipping his top hat and gazing towards the vaulted ceiling of the circus tent.

In their glittering gold leotards, a man and two women swung high above the crowd, twisting and flipping acrobatically while the audience watched in amazement.

"Have you ever seen anything so spectacular?" Sasha murmured to her best friend, Yasmin, from the stands, and Yasmin shook her head.

Just then, both women let go of their trapezes, launching themselves into synchronized somersaults before the man caught them both in mid-air.

The crowd burst into uncontrollable

applause, but no one was more excited than Sasha, who leaped to her feet, whistling and cheering until her throat grew hoarse.

"Well, I think I can guess what Sasha's favourite part of the circus was," Jade joked to her best friend, Cloe.

As the four friends filed out of the circus tent, Sasha couldn't stop talking about the trapeze artists. "Can you believe how utterly fearless they were up there?" she gushed. "Did you see those flips they did?"

"They were kind of hard to miss," Jade teased.

"Well, they are totally my new role models," Sasha announced. She looped her arms through her best friends' arms to keep them from getting separated and losing each other in the crowd.

"Um, I thought you wanted to be a record producer – not a circus performer," Cloe replied, swerving to avoid a gaggle of giggling

school kids who pushed past the girls.

"Hey, a good role model can come from any walk of life," Sasha explained. "I mean, mastering moves like those takes serious dedication and skill!"

"True ... but it's also seriously scary stuff!" Cloe pointed out.

Sasha just shrugged. She was always up for pushing herself to the limit, so the thought of flying through the air on a trapeze really didn't freak her out.

"So what's the deal, Sash?" Yasmin asked. "Are you planning to run off and join the circus?"

"Not exactly," Sasha said thoughtfully.

Her friends looked at each other in

confusion. "Seriously, you can't run away and join the circus!" Cloe cried.

"Don't worry, I won't do *that*," Sasha assured them. "Now come on – I need my new role models' autographs!"

Sasha led them towards the stage door, where they waited patiently, talking about all the amazing acts they had seen, until the Soaring Santinis appeared. Sasha rushed up to them, gushing about how much she admired their skill, and they happily signed her program.

"If you like the trapeze so much, you should learn to ride it yourself!" the brunette Santini sister told her.

"Maybe I will," Sasha agreed. As the girls weaved their way through the car park and piled into Jade's VW Bug, her friends kept shooting glances at her, trying to guess what new scheme she had in mind. Sasha always came up with the best ideas, and they couldn't

wait to see what she would do next!

The next morning, Sasha strutted into the school cafeteria in a totally adorable new outfit — a burgundy ruffled shirt, a wrap-around, embroidered denim skirt, a wide black belt and cute striped tights with strappy heels.

"Whoa, Sasha, what inspired the new look?" Yasmin asked, tugging playfully at one of the pigtails her friend had tamed her normally loose hair into.

"I like to think of it as 'circus chic'," Sasha explained, "and it's in honour of my recent enrollment at the Stilesville School of Circus Arts to learn all kinds of new tricks!"

"We have a school of circus arts?" Jade asked, looking skeptical. She didn't exactly expect a small town like Stilesville to offer the very best in circus training.

"We do," Sasha confirmed. "One of the top acrobats from the Sterling Sisters Circus

retired right here in Stilesville a few years ago and decided to start her own school."

"How cool!" Yasmin cried as she led the way into their drama class. "So you'll be learning how to do all of those amazing trapeze tricks?"

"Yep," Sasha replied. "But they have classes in lots of other awesome circus arts too. So I might dabble in all of them."

"Sasha!" exclaimed their drama teacher, Ms Hall, rushing over to the girls. "How did you know the play I've just chosen for our spring production is *Under the Big Top*? You look born to play a part in that outfit!"

Their teacher looked admiringly at Sasha's circus-inspired outfit.

"I didn't – but now that I'm officially a student of the circus arts, I bet I'd be great at any of the parts!" Sasha declared, taking her seat at the front of the classroom.

"Ooh, I bet you would," Ms Hall said happily. "I can't wait to see your audition!"

"Are you really going to have time for the spring play and your new circus classes and everything else you already do?" Yasmin whispered to Sasha once they were all sitting around their usual table.

"I'll figure it out," Sasha replied with a shrug. "I always do."

CHAPTER 2

That night, Sasha arrived at her very first trapeze class in the leotard, tights and jazz shoes she usually wore for her dance classes.

"Welcome!" exclaimed a short, slender woman with her long brown hair wound into a French twist. "I am The Amazing Anjelica – but you can just call me Anjeli."

"Great to meet you!" Sasha rushed over and enthusiastically shook the teacher's hand. "I've been researching you online, and wow, what a spectacular career you've had! I mean, its almost unbelievable!"

"That's why they call her 'amazing'," pointed out a girl so pale she looked like she was made of porcelain.

"And that's why she's the boss!" added another student, taller and more tanned than the others but still incredibly fit. "I'm Kylie, by the way."

"And this is Meadow," their teacher said, gesturing to the blonde girl who had spoken first. Sasha held out her hand, which the smaller girl shook limply.

"We try to keep our classes small, but we do have two more students, who should be arriving any minute," Anjelica continued.

Just then, two girls burst through the door, hair, bags and coats flying behind them as they hurried to get inside.

"Are we late?" gasped one girl, brushing her curly hair out of her eyes.

"Please say we're not late!" cried the other, her sleek black ponytail bouncing.

"And these are Cadence and Saffron," their teacher finished, gesturing to first one girl, then the other. "And now that you ladies have decided to join us, why don't we get you all warmed-up and ready to go?"

The girls lined up, and Meadow whispered to Sasha, "Aren't you cold in that?"

Sasha glanced around and noticed that all the other girls wore spandex pants over their leotards. "I'll manage." But she shivered a little – it was a *bit* cold in the studio – and decided that she would definitely dress more like the other girls for the next lesson.

Anjelica led the girls through a series of warm-ups that were a lot like the ones Sasha did in her dance classes, focusing on upper body stretches. Sasha started to feel like this wouldn't be so hard after all.

But then Anjelica released six low-flying trapezes from their hooks so they all dangled in the centre of the room, and Sasha remembered that this was not like anything she had ever tried before.

"Now, Sasha, these girls are a little more advanced than you, but for safety's sake, I'll

run through some basics for you before we begin." Her teacher handed her a trapeze, which hung only a few feet off the ground. "Grasp the bar with both hands, about shoulder-width apart," she began.

Beside her, Sasha heard Meadow mutter to Cadence, "I can't *believe* we have to sit through all of this again."

"I know, right?" Cadence agreed, but Sasha ignored them, focusing on her teacher's instructions instead.

"Now you need to support yourself using your upper body to keep your feet off the ground," Anjelica continued, and Sasha did as she said.

The other girls followed suit, though they kept grumbling about having to go over all this again.

"Begin by swinging your legs forward, and then back, making sure that you're controlling the movement, keeping your legs straight and your toes pointed," Anjelica instructed.

Sasha lifted her legs forwards, then launched them back behind her, and a smile spread across her face. Even though she was barely off the ground, she already felt like she was flying! Out of the corner of her eye, she saw her classmates also swinging through the air beside her. Despite their complaints and their negativity, all of them seemed to be having fun too.

"Good!" Anjelica cried. "Now we're going to try the same thing, but using the high platform." She gestured upward, and Sasha's eyes widened at the sight of the platform at the top of a ladder with a trapeze hanging in front of it. Sasha had never been afraid of heights, but then she had never before been dangling in mid-air with only a bar to hold on to, either!

Sasha watched as each of the other girls took a turn, flying from one side of the room

to the other, swinging their legs just as they had on the low trapeze.

They all looked utterly relaxed, not at all frightened, so although Sasha felt her stomach tighten into a nervous knot as her turn approached, she strived to keep her expression calm.

"That looked amazing!" she told the other girls.

"Thanks!" Kylie replied, though the others didn't answer.

Sasha slowly climbed the ladder, meeting Anjelica on the wooden platform at the top. Her teacher expertly fastened a sturdy safety rope

around her waist, then held the trapeze steady. With the balls of her feet at the edge of the ledge, Sasha leaned forward and grasped the bar just as she had the low trapeze, breathing deeply to control her nerves.

"Don't look at the ground!" her teacher reminded her, and Sasha nodded. "Look forwards and you'll go forwards!"

"Now, to prepare you, I'll say, 'ready, set, hep!'" Anjelica explained. "On 'set', bend your legs, and on 'hep', jump up into the air with your arms straight in front of you and your legs slightly forward. Then as you're swinging, I'll tell you when to hold your legs up, when to swing them back, and when to bring them forward again. Ready?"

Sasha nodded again, a serious look on her face. "Ready."

"Set!" her teacher cried, and Sasha bent her knees. "Hep!" Sasha hopped up and swung forwards, arcing across the studio, feeling the

wind whip through her ponytail.

"Legs up!" she heard Anjelica shout behind her, and Sasha swung her legs forward, already feeling the momentum of her swing beginning to pull her back towards the platform. "And back!" her teacher called, and Sasha swung her legs behind her. "Now forwards!" Anjelica told her almost immediately, as Sasha reached the high point of her backswing. Sasha brought her legs forwards once more, laughing at the sheer joy of flying through the air.

She repeated the motions through a couple more swings, and then Anjelica called, "Ready, set, hep!" again. As Anjelica had told her to do, Sasha let go of the trapeze on 'hep', and her teacher lowered her by her safety rope to the mat below.

"Wow!" Sasha gasped. "That was incredible!" She unhooked her safety rope and turned to watch Anjelica climbing down the ladder. "Can I go again?"

Anjelica laughed softly. "That's how everyone feels after they fly the first time. But actually, that's all the time we have for today. Don't worry, though – there will be lots more trapeze practise next time! And if you sign up for our circus camp here over winter break, you can practise on the trapeze all day if you want to!"

"I'm totally there!" Sasha couldn't stop smiling as she shrugged into her coat, grabbed her bag, and headed for the door. She was blown away by the buzz she'd got from the trapeze, but also from the knowledge that she really could do anything if she just went for it and reached for the stars.

"Hey, that was really great for your first time," Kylie said, catching up to her.

"Well, *that's* not the hard part," Saffron pointed out, edging past them with Cadence and Meadow at her side.

"Don't mind them," Kylie whispered once the other girls were past.

"Oh, I don't," Sasha assured her.

"It's just, ever since they decided they're going to become professional trapeze artists, it's like they think they're too good for anyone else," Kylie explained.

Sasha looked at the taller girl in surprise. "Really? They're planning to go pro? Wow, that's amazing."

"Oh, yeah," Kylie told her. "They've even got a name all picked out – the Aerial Angels, after our teacher."

"They don't exactly seem angelic to me," Sasha muttered, and her new friend grinned back at her.

"I'd have to agree with you there!" Kylie replied as they strolled outside together. "So that's why I'm glad you joined this class – you seem way nicer than those girls!"

"Right back at you," Sasha said. She paused to look at a flyer posted by the front door,

advertising the school's "Winter Wonderland of Circus Arts Camp," and smiled. "You know what? I bet I can tip the nice-girl balance in this class in our favour!"

CHAPTER 3

"You *have* to try it," Sasha told her best friends at lunch the next day.

"That sounds so scary!" Yasmin replied.

"But awesome!" Jade added. "Sign me up, Bunny Boo!"

"Actually, there's a circus arts camp over winter break that I thought all of you might enjoy," Sasha continued. "We'll be trained in all sorts of circus acts, like animal training, magic and clowning – plus trapeze of course! And then we'll all perform in our own circus at the school."

"Ooh, that sounds like fun!" Cloe squealed, as she clapped her hands in delight.

"And don't worry, Yas," Sasha said. "You don't even have to try the trapeze if you don't want to. You can focus on one of the other circus acts if you want."

"Animal training *does* sound pretty cool," Yasmin admitted.

"I bet I would make a fabulous magician," Jade chimed in. "After all, I work fashion magic on a daily basis!"

She hopped up from the table and struck a pose in her capris and ruffled top to demonstrate. "Am I right?"

Her friends all nodded their agreement.

"You know, I think I would make a totally adorable clown," Cloe announced.

"You certainly know how to take a fall," Jade teased, making Cloe blush. Cloe's friends found her klutziness endearing, but it was sometimes quite embarrassing for her.

"That's true," Cloe admitted. "But I do think I could be really funny!"

"Of course you could," Yasmin assured her, smiling at her friend.

"So what do you say, girls?" Sasha asked. "Should we all go to circus camp and rock it?"

Jade and Cloe nodded eagerly, but Yasmin looked uncertain. Her friends all turned to her, and after a long moment she agreed, "Okay. Let's do it."

The bell rang, and the girls dumped their lunch trays into the bin before heading to drama class, where Ms Hall was encouraging everyone to sign up for spring play auditions. "They're

right after winter break, so you'll have plenty of time to prepare," she explained.

"Wow, I can't believe it's the last day of school before winter break already," Yasmin told her friends.

"Yeah, and I can't wait!" Cloe cried. She grabbed a pen and scrawled her name at the top of the audition sign-up sheet. "So, what do you say, girls?" she asked hopefully. "Wanna try out for the play when we get back from being circus stars?"

"Looks like you've made up your mind already," Jade teased, taking the pen from her friend and signing up as well. "But yeah, it sounds like fun."

"But will we really have time to get ready for our auditions if we're spending our whole break at circus camp?" Yasmin reminded them. "It sounds pretty intense!"

"I was born ready!" Cloe declared, raising her arms in the air and throwing her head back

in what her friends thought of as her diva pose.

"Of course you were, Angel," Jade replied, laughing at her friend's dramatic nature.

"I hope you girls are practising your monologues over here," Ms Hall interrupted, and the girls all quickly turned their attention to the pieces they were supposed to be practising for class, though now that Sasha had brought it up, the circus was all they could think about.

Sasha led the girls into the Stilesville School of Circus Arts after school and paraded them into Anjelica's office.

"I have some new students for you!" she exclaimed, before noticing that Saffron and Cadence were sitting in the office already, looking very serious.

"Would you mind waiting for just a moment?" Anjelica smiled at Sasha and her friends as they hurried out of the room, but

Sasha could feel the heat of the other girls' glares as she retreated.

"Well, they seemed nice," Jade joked.

"Meet my classmates," Sasha grumbled. "This is exactly why I need you girls here!"

"Yeah, I can see that," Yasmin replied. "Are they all that unfriendly?"

"Mostly," Sasha admitted, taking a seat in the circus school's lobby. "But there's one nice girl. And soon there'll be all of you!"

"We are world-renowned for our niceness," Jade agreed, plopping into a beautiful plush chair next to Sasha.

"And soon we'll be world-renowned for our circus skills!" Cloe vowed.

While she was speaking, Cadence and Saffron strutted out of Anjelica's office, and both girls smirked at Cloe's words. "Yeah, I'm sure," Saffron scoffed.

"We will!" Cloe shouted after them,

infuriated by their snottiness. But the girls didn't even glance back at her as they sashayed out through the door.

"See what I mean?" Sasha murmured, and her friends all nodded.

"Do they go to Stilesville High?" Yasmin asked. "I don't recognize them."

"Nope – they go to Stilesville West," Sasha replied. "Which is apparently all the more reason they won't speak to me."

Anjelica appeared in the doorway of her office and motioned the girls in. "Come in, come in!" she called. Once they were all seated on the comfy couch opposite her desk, she asked, "What can I do for you ladies?"

"These are my best friends, and they all want to sign up for your circus camp!" Sasha blurted out.

"Well, that's wonderful!" Anjelica beamed at all four girls. "Do you all know what you'd like to focus on yet?"

They told her: clowning for Cloe, magic for Jade, animal training for Yasmin and, of course, the trapeze for Sasha. As each girl spoke and their enthusiam shone through, Anjelica's smile just got bigger and bigger.

"Sounds like you girls have all the acts you need to form your very own circus!" she exclaimed, still beaming.

"Really?" Cloe gasped, leaning forwards eagerly.

"Absolutely," Anjelica assured her. "You girls will be strutting your stuff under the big top in no time, I'm sure of it!"

After signing up for the winter break camp, the girls hurried back to Sasha's car, chattering excitedly about the weeks ahead.

"Just think of all the amazing things we'll be able to do by the time school starts again!" Cloe cried.

"Maybe we can start our own Stilesville High Circus," Yasmin suggested.

"Or better yet, our own circus, period," Sasha replied. "Just the four of us, taking centre stage across the globe!"

"That *does* sound cool," Jade agreed. "But do you think four people are enough to create a whole circus?"

"Sure," Sasha said with a shrug. "I mean, we're all multi-talented, right? So we can totally pull it off!"

"You know, when we went to the circus, I really never thought we might be doing the same thing one day," Yasmin pointed out. "But now we will be in, like, a week! Sometimes I just can't believe how lucky we really are."

"And it just goes to show, you never know where your next big idea will come from," Sasha told her as they all slipped into the car.

"Or where your next adventure will take you!" Cloe added. As they drove back to Sasha's house to hang out, the girls couldn't stop talking about the circus camp and all the amazing things they would get to try there.

CHAPTER 4

On the first day of winter break, Sasha and her friends arrived at the School of Circus Arts, ready to try anything in their cropped yoga pants and tank tops.

"All right, ladies, we've got lots to do, so let's get started!" Anjelica exclaimed.

All eight students followed her as she led them on a tour of the school, introducing them to each of their instructors as they went. "We've got a wonderful group of teachers here," Anjelica told them. "In fact, they were all in the Sterling Circus with me and we toured the world together!"

"Wow – how did you get them all to stick around here in Stilesville?" Yasmin asked.

"Stilesville was one of our favourite stops

on our tour," Anjelica explained. "So when we got tired of touring all the time, we thought this would be the perfect place to share our arts with others!"

"Well, I'm seriously glad you did," Sasha told her.

They started their tour in the beautiful stables at the back of the building, where Yasmin was thrilled to meet the two white show horses they would be practising trick riding on. "These are Snowflake and Moonlight," their riding instructor, The Incredible Isabelle, explained.

Smiling, Yasmin patted each horse's velvety white nose. "We're going to have so much fun together!" she murmured to the horses.

"Check it out – she's way better with animals than with people," Cadence muttered to her friends, and they all hid sniggers behind their hands.

"That is a very good trait in an animal trainer," Isabelle interrupted in her soft accent. "I often think that I am better with my animals than with people, too. Animals tend to be so much nicer!"

"Certainly nicer than some people," Jade agreed, shooting a glare at Cadence, Meadow and Saffron.

"I'd love to have you start here with me," Isabelle told Yasmin, who nodded eagerly.

"*I'm* a champion horseback rider," Meadow interrupted. "So I'll start here too, okay?"

"Of course," Isabelle replied.

"I'll bring them right back," Anjelica promised as they moved on to the next stop on their tour.

"Meet The Marvelous Marlin," she declared as they stepped into a classroom, and a tall, thin man dressed all in black took a bow.

"At your service," he said in a deep, velvety voice.

"Oooh, totally mystical," Jade whispered to her friends.

"Who's ready to work some magic?" Marlin asked, and Jade stepped forward, barely able to contain her excitement.

"I am!" she squealed.

"Too bad no one worked any magic on *her*," Saffron said, making her friends giggle again.

"Jade, I take it you'll be starting your training with Marlin?" Anjelica asked, trying to drown out her student's rude comment.

"That would be amazing!" Jade replied.

"I wouldn't mind trying my hand at magic too," Kylie chimed in. Jade looked relieved that she had been paired with their one friendly classmate.

"We'll be back in a flash," Anjelica promised, ushering the girls into the theatre down the hall.

"And here's Merry Marisol, the funniest clown around!" she announced, as a short blonde woman in a flared pink dress did a little twirl on the stage in front of them.

"So, who's joining me for the most fun class in this whole camp?" Marisol asked, turning her huge, sunny smile on all of the students.

"Ooh, I am!" Cloe squealed.

Meanwhile, Saffron and Cadence seemed to be involved in a dispute. "You do it!" Saffron hissed, looking displeased that Cadence had disagreed with her in any way.

"No, you!" Cadence insisted. "I *have* to focus on trapeze – I'm the lead performer in our act after all!"

"Fine," Saffron sighed. She turned to Marisol and flashed a fake smile. "I'll be joining your class, too."

"Wow, that was enthusiastic," Jade murmured to Cloe.

Cloe looked worriedly at her friends – she didn't want to deal with Saffron making fun of her the whole time she was trying to learn how to be a totally hilarious clown.

"Well, I guess that leaves Sasha and Cadence with me," Anjelica announced. "And remember, you'll all get a shot at every one of these classes over today and tomorrow, so don't worry if you didn't get your first choice just now!" At that, she shot a pointed look at Saffron. "After you've sampled everything, you'll get to pick a speciality for the rest of the camp."

"I know what I *won't* be picking," Saffron complained, and Cloe sighed. It was going to be a long morning.

The four best friends wished each other luck before heading off to their separate classes. They couldn't wait to learn all sorts of cool new things, but they wished they could be in better company while they did it.

CHAPTER 5

"Will we get to learn about training any other types of animals in this class?" Yasmin asked once she was back in the stable.

"Hopefully we'll have time for that," Isabelle told her. "But for now, let's get to know these horses!"

"I'd love to," Yasmin agreed.

"Um, you *have* ridden a horse before, haven't you?" Meadow demanded.

"Of course I have," Yasmin informed her. "But I'm assuming circus riding is just a little bit different."

"It certainly is," Isabelle replied. "Although the first step is the same: you need to get to know your horse."

"Okay, we've already met them, so what's step two?" Meadow interrupted.

"You cannot rush horse training," Isabelle said sternly. "You have to be gentle with these horses and speak softly to them. And a few sugar cubes don't hurt, either." She pulled a handful of sugar cubes out of her pocket and passed them out to each of her students.

"Who needs sugar cubes?" Meadow scoffed. "Well-trained horses do what they're told, and that's all there is to it."

"Oh, I can assure you that my horses are well trained," Isabelle informed her. "These are professional circus horses, used to performing in front of huge crowds. But that doesn't mean they'll be willing to perform for *you*."

While their teacher gave Meadow a talking-to, Yasmin was speaking softly to Snowflake. "Hey, Snow-baby," she murmured. "You're a good horsey, aren't you?" She held a sugar cube out on the palm of her hand with her fingers stretched flat to

keep them out of the horse's way, and offered the cube to her new animal friend. Snowflake gobbled it up eagerly. Yasmin began gently stroking Snowflake's white head, and the horse snuffled happily in response.

Turning away from her difficult student, Isabelle noticed Yasmin busily bonding with the horse. "Looks like you have won her trust already!" the teacher declared. "Meadow, why don't you try doing the same?"

Meadow rolled her eyes and sashayed over to Moonlight. "Hey, horse. Want some sugar?" She held out a sugar cube and the horse snatched it up, eyeing her warily as he did. Looking annoyed, she tried to pat the horse's head, but he pulled away, looking frightened and tense. Isabelle took a step towards Meadow, looking concerned.

"What is this horse's problem?" Meadow demanded. "I wanna switch — Yasmin snagged the good horse! I don't stand a chance with this one."

"Both of these horses have had identical training," Isabelle replied. "The difference here is clearly in their current trainers." She stared pointedly at Meadow until the girl looked away, her white-blonde pageboy haircut falling over her pale cheeks and hiding her ice-blue eyes.

"It is vital that a circus horse has absolute confidence in their rider," Isabelle explained, talking now to Yasmin while Meadow sulked. "There are many things that go on in a circus ring that might startle a horse — loud noises, flashing lights, fluttering costumes. But if you make the horse feel safe and calm, they will face anything for you."

"That's exactly how I feel about my best friends," Yasmin told her. "No matter what's going on, I know that with them at my side, I'll be okay."

"Um, this horse isn't your best friend," Meadow informed her, sounding irritated.

"But it should be!" Isabelle declared. "These two horses are certainly among my best friends. And if you're going to spend as much time with a horse as it takes to properly train it, it really helps if you become good friends in the process."

"So, are we gonna get to ride at all?" Meadow interrupted. "I mean, standing around the stalls is fun and all, but there's not that much more we can learn without actually getting on the horse, is there?"

"For once, Meadow is right," Isabelle announced. "We'll learn much more about how you interact with these horses once you're in the ring. So let's get started!"

She led the girls to the tack room, and showed them where the bridles and English-style saddles were kept for each horse.

Back in the stalls, she watched closely as each girl swung the saddle onto her horse's back and cinched it around the horse's belly,

before gently guiding the metal bit of the bridle into the horse's mouth and slipping the headpiece over its ears.

"Well done, girls," she called, sounding impressed. "Now, let's get them into the ring, shall we?"

She held the stall doors open as the girls led their horses out. Yasmin, Meadow and their horses followed Isabelle into the indoor ring where they would be practising, its floor covered with sawdust.

"Now, many circus riders don't even use a saddle or bridle," Isabelle explained. "But I like to start my students out with them, and maybe eventually you can try some tricks without them as you progress."

As the girls swung onto their horses' backs, Meadow called, "I'm ready to try it now, I'm a champion rider!"

"No," Isabelle informed her. "You aren't."

Meadow didn't have much time to pout atop her horse before their teacher started putting them through their paces, first walking, then trotting, then cantering their horses around the ring.

"Good control!" Isabelle shouted to be heard over the horses' pounding hooves. "Now, are you ready to try a gallop?"

"Yeah!" the girls both cried as they flew around the ring on their horses' backs.

"Ask them to go faster," Isabelle told them, and both girls nudged their horses' sides until they sped up into a gallop, a horse's fastest gait. "Remember to keep plenty of room between the two of you – the ring is not that big!"

Yasmin loved feeling like she was one with the horse as Snowflake carried her swiftly around the corral. But suddenly she heard hoof beats immediately behind her, and glanced back to see that Meadow and Moonlight were getting entirely too close, and not slowing down at all.

"Pull back on the reins, Meadow!" Isabelle yelled, but Meadow seemed to be having trouble getting her horse to listen to her.

It looked like the horses were about to collide! But just in time, Yasmin guided her horse into the centre of the ring, where they stood waiting while Meadow gradually slowed her horse to a walk and finally a stop.

"I'm sorry," Meadow gasped, her voice shaking with fear. "I'd forgotten how fast a gallop could be!"

"That could have been a very bad accident, for both you and the horses," Isabelle said. "But thanks to Yasmin's quick thinking, it was avoided."

"Yeah," Meadow whispered, "thanks, Yasmin."

Yasmin nodded modestly as their teacher continued, "If you're ever going to be a circus rider, you must control your competitive spirit to ensure that you and your horse are working together with the other riders and horses in the ring. Do you understand?"

"Yes," Meadow murmured. "I'll be more careful next time."

Isabelle gave her student a long, searching look, before finally nodding, apparently satisfied that Meadow would not make the same mistake again. "Good. Now let's try that again. You can both do it if you put your minds to work."

The girls led their horses to the edge of the ring, and urged them into a gallop once more, but this time, Meadow made sure that her horse kept an even pace with Yasmin's, rather than trying to race her around the ring.

CHAPTER 6

"Do you believe in magic?" Marlin asked Jade and Kylie back in his magician's studio.

The girls looked at each other uncertainly, and Jade finally answered, "Well, sort of. I mean, I'd like to."

Marlin's long, serious face broke into a smile. "Good answer! I would love to believe in magic, too, but the magic I do is strictly tricks and illusions. Which are fun too!"

He motioned the girls over to his trunk of magic tricks, which was painted purple and decorated with stars.

"I like your sense of style!" Jade declared, looking admiringly at the box.

"Wait till you see what's inside!" He opened the lid and revealed his collection of cards, coins, juggling balls, multicoloured scarves, metal rings, fake flowers and more, all crammed together yet carefully organized to make them easy to find.

"Wow," Kylie murmured. "Doing magic takes a lot of stuff!"

"It sure does," Marlin agreed, laughing.

"Are we going to learn how to pull a rabbit out of a hat, or make it look like we've cut someone in half?" Jade asked excitedly. "I've always wanted to know how to do those tricks, they're why I love magic so much!"

"We will," Marlin promised. "But first, let's start with a card trick, the basic tool for any magician."

He grabbed a deck of cards from his trunk and fanned them out on the table in front of the girls. They both leaned forward,

eager to see what he would do next. But he paused, gazing at both of them intently. "Are you sure you want to learn the secrets to these magic tricks? Because once you do, I guarantee you'll never look at a magic show the same way again."

"Definitely!" Jade cried.

"Absolutely," Kylie agreed.

"Okay then." The magician smiled, picked up the cards, and held them out towards Jade. "Pick a card, any card."

She chose a card from the middle of the deck, and he continued, "Look at it, remember what it is, but don't show it to me at all."

Jade glanced at the card and saw that it was the three of hearts. "Now, give the card back to me," he said, and she handed the card over. He slipped it back into the deck.

"Now, I will reveal your card!" He counted off cards until he reached number seven, then flipped the eighth over and asked, "Is that your card?"

Jade stared at him in amazement – he had turned over her card, the three of hearts! "How did you do that?" she gasped.

"Any guesses?" he inquired, and the girls shook their heads.

"It's actually pretty simple, once you know how it works," he explained. "I just count off the top seven cards, and when I put the card back in the deck, I make sure to place it under the seventh one. That way, whatever your card is, I can find it with no problem."

"How cool!" Kylie cried. "Can I please try?"

"Of course," Marlin agreed. "This is a class, after all!" He handed the deck over to her, then she shuffled the cards before carefully counting off the top seven.

"Now, remember, the audience can't notice that you're counting cards in advance, or they'll be suspicious," he told her. "Magic is all about subtlety."

Kylie nodded and shuffled the cards again. This time, when she separated out the cards, it wasn't noticeable at all.

"Pick a card," she said, holding the deck out to Jade. Once again, Jade selected a card from the deck, looked at it, then handed it back to Kylie.

"Make sure you make it look like you're putting the card back in a random spot," Marlin added. "The trick will be obvious if your audience can see that you put the card back in a specific place, and the illusion will be ruined."

Kylie slid the card back into the deck, careful not to obviously hold the first seven cards apart. "One, two, three, four, five, six, seven!" she counted, before turning over the eighth card to reveal the seven of clubs. "Is that your card?"

"Yep!" Jade replied. "Good job, Kylie!" Turning to their teacher, she added, "Okay, now do we get our capes, wands, hats and bunnies?"

Grinning, Marlin replied, "Soon, I promise. But first, let's try a coin trick, the second essential type of trick any magician has to know."

He leaned over his trunk, rummaged through it, then sat up and held up two pennies. "Two normal coins, right?" They both nodded. "But now I'm going to rub them together to make a third one appear!"

He set one coin on top of the other, then rubbed them so fast between his thumb and

forefinger that it looked like there were three coins there.

"So it's an optical illusion, right?" Kylie asked, almost sounding a little disappointed.

"Is it?" Marlin closed his fist around the coins, then reopened it to reveal three pennies lying in the palm of his hand.

"Wow, multiplying money — now there's a trick I could use!" Jade exclaimed. "But maybe next time you could try it with something bigger, like maybe a silver dollar?"

"If this really were a way to make extra cash appear, believe me, I would," Marlin assured her. "But I actually had a third coin hidden in my hand the whole time."

"No way!" Jade protested. "Where was it, Marlin?"

"Squeezed between the base of my thumb and my palm, where you couldn't see it," he told her. "That's the best spot to hide a coin

anytime you need to for a trick. Jade, do you want to try?"

When she nodded, he handed all three coins over to her. "First, you need to hide the third coin without anyone noticing."

Jade put her hands in her lap, then raised them above the table and held up two pennies. "Ready to watch me make money?" she asked playfully. She rubbed the coins together quickly, making it look like there was a third one between them, just like Marlin had done.

"There aren't really three coins there!" Marlin cried, pretending to be a typical audience member.

"Oh, yes there are!" Jade closed her hand, then opened it and showed the others that she held three coins. Kylie burst into applause. Turning to her teacher, Jade asked, "How did I do?"

"Great!" he assured her. "Fantastic showmanship – you almost made *me* believe you'd made money!"

Jade smiled, looking proud of herself. "Who knew cards and coins could be so amazing?" she asked.

"And it only gets better from there!" Marlin added. "I'll teach you how to read minds, make things disappear and all sorts of cool stuff!"

"Including making a rabbit appear in a hat?" Jade insisted.

"Of course," Marlin agreed. "No magic show would be complete without a rabbit!"

He led the girls over to the rabbit hutch in the corner of the room, where a cute, fuzzy white rabbit peered back at them, its whiskers twitching rapidly.

"This is Magic," he told the girls. "Magic the Bunny, meet Jade and Kylie. They'll soon be making you disappear too!"

Jade reached into the rabbit's cage and stroked his downy soft head. "He's adorable!" she squealed. "And I do think he looks a little magical, too."

"Oh, he is," Marlin assured her. "But before you're ready for the big bunny trick, why don't we try a few simpler ones?"

"I'm up for that," Kylie replied, looking at the rabbit uncertainly. "I'm not sure I'm ready to handle live animals yet!"

"Well, that's the great thing about magic — there are so many different types of tricks you can do, so if one kind isn't your thing, there are plenty of others to choose from," Marlin told her.

"So I don't have to do the rabbit trick?" Kylie asked.

"Definitely not," Marlin said, making Kylie smile with relief.

"So, what's the next trick?" Jade interrupted, eager to learn more tricks.

"How would you like to learn how to levitate?" their teacher suggested, and the girls squealed.

"Ooh, that sounds amazing!" Jade cried.

"Amazing is what we aim for!" Marlin announced as he started to demonstrate the first moves of his next big trick.

CHAPTER 7

"You are just *sooo* funny," Saffron cooed after Marisol demonstrated her clumsy juggling routine in the clown studio.

Cloe sighed – even though the other girl hadn't even wanted to join the clown class, she kept trying to butter their teacher up.

"Well, thank you," Marisol replied, giving the girls a quick curtsey. "And you can be too! Now, the first thing you need to do is pick a fun clown name. That'll help you figure out your clown persona."

"Can I be Cutie Cloe?" Cloe suggested. "I could put my hair in pigtails and wear a babydoll dress. What do you think?"

"I think that's great!" Marisol agreed.

"Um, wouldn't you actually need to be cute to make that name work?" Saffron muttered under her breath, so only Cloe could hear her properly.

"What's that, Saffron?" their teacher asked.

"Oh, I said I think my name should be Saffron Sweetie," Saffron replied. "Will that work do you think?"

"Hmm ... that sounds a lot like Cloe's name," Marisol began, "but sure, it'll do for now I guess."

Saffron gave Cloe an angry look, but then turned a sugary smile on for Marisol.

"Now, you need to think about who your character is and what her personality is like," Marisol continued, "so I want you to take a few minutes to write about what type of clown you think you'd like to be."

"But I'm totally not a good writer!" Cloe protested.

"*I* am," Saffron interjected. "This is an *awesome* assignment!"

"Don't worry, Cloe," her teacher said. "I won't even read it. It's just a good way for you to develop your clown character, for your own information."

"Okay," Cloe agreed, but she still sounded unsure. She sat down in an overstuffed chair in the corner, pulled her sketchpad out of her bag, and started writing. At first the words came slowly, but once she got started, she was surprised at how much she had to say about her character. "Cutie is sweet, curious, and childlike. She loves making new friends and discovering new things. She's easily confused and very clumsy."

As the ideas flowed out of her, she began to smile – she could really see this character coming to life in her imagination!

After a moment, their instructor asked, "Okay, girls, do you feel like you know what kind of clown you want to be?"

"Maybe ..." Saffron looked nervous as she stared down at the page she had written.

"It's okay – it'll become clearer once you've practised your act a little," Marisol assured the girls. "This is just a starting point."

"This totally helped me figure out who my character is," Cloe announced. "You know, I *love* acting, but I've never got to make up my own character before. This is so much fun!"

"Then you'll love our next exercise," Marisol told her. "Let's try sketching out clown costumes and makeup. See, clowning is a visual medium, so the audience's first impression is all about how you look, move and act."

"Ohmigosh, this just gets better and better!" Cloe squealed. "I get to be a fashion and make-up designer too? Being a clown involves everything I love!"

"It's a pretty fun job," Marisol agreed.

Hardly able to contain her excitement, Cloe grabbed a set of coloured pencils out of her bag and hunched over her sketchpad. She rapidly sketched a couple of different looks, but soon she arrived at her favourite: a ruffled hot-pink dress with black-and-white diamond patterned tights, strappy black heels tied with fuchsia ribbons, long black gloves, a little black hat cocked at a jaunty angle, and pink hoop earrings.

To make it a little more clownlike, she drew in bright pink blush on the cheeks, added pretty pink lipstick, and outlined the eyes in black accented with sparkly lavender eyeshadow.

She sat back and admired her drawing, then hopped up and ran over to Marisol. "How's this look?" she asked, holding her sketchpad out to her teacher.

"Cloe, that's perfect!" Marisol exclaimed. "I can totally see you stealing the spotlight under the big top in this outfit!"

"Really?" Cloe squealed. "You think it works for me?"

"Absolutely!" her teacher cried. "You're going to make an utterly amazing clown." Glancing at her other student, she asked, "And what did you come up with?"

"I'm still working." Saffron covered her page with her arm to hide her sketches.

"No problem," Marisol assured her. "But why don't you come back to that later? For now, let's try some pantomime to get you into clowning mode and help build up your confidence."

Both girls set aside their drawings and stood up, awaiting their teacher's instructions.

"I want you girls to practise some silly walks," she began. "Take turns walking across the room, doing a different funny walk each time. Ready? Go!"

Cloe went first, and did a bunny hop from one side of the room to the other. Next Saffron acted like she was swimming through the air, then Cloe high-stepped across the studio, and Saffron took a turn zigzagging back and forth.

"Cool moves, girls!" Marisol declared. "Now, let's try pretending to walk through different environments. I'll give you each one to try, and then the other one will guess where she's supposed to be."

She motioned Cloe over and whispered, "Pretend you're walking down a windy, rainy street." Cloe nodded and took her place at

the far end of the room. With a deep breath, she strode across the studio, leaning back like she was being blown away by the wind but still struggled forward, wiping at her face like water was dripping into her eyes, and shielding her head to protect it from the imaginary rain.

"Walking through a rainstorm!" Saffron guessed, and Cloe nodded happily.

"Okay, Saffron, your turn." Marisol gestured for Saffron to come over, and whispered, "Pretend you're walking across a giant bouncy castle."

Saffron began bounding across the room, making exaggerated gestures with her arms and legs, and Cloe cried, "Ooh, crossing a floor made of springs, right?"

"Right!" Saffron stopped and pointed at Cloe in excitement, forgetting for a moment that she wasn't supposed to like her classmate, or the clown class.

"Good job!" Marisol applauded for her students. "Now, I want you to try doing different things in character. Cutie Cloe, let's see you pick some flowers."

Cloe leaned way over and pretended to examine a bunch of flowers, but she leaned too far and tipped over, windmilling her arms as she took a pratfall.

She heard Saffron and Marisol laughing, and although she was excited that her first clown trick had been a success, she maintained her focus and kept going with her act.

Picking herself up, she turned and leaned over again, then pretended to pluck a few blooms and gather them in one hand. Smiling, she frolicked across the room, pausing to sniff her bouquet as she went. When she reached the end of the room, she whirled around and took a bow as her teacher and classmate clapped.

"You have that character down to a pat!" Marisol declared. "Now, Saffron Sweetie, how would you ride a bike?"

Saffron paused, looking nervous, then swung her leg into the air and began raising one leg after the other as if she were riding a bike. But then she stopped, sighed, and admitted, "I don't know what else to do! I didn't want to do this class because I don't know how to be funny!"

"It's okay," Marisol assured her. "It isn't easy! With practise, anyone can be a fabulous clown, trust me."

"Not me," Saffron sighed. She sagged to the ground, her shiny black hair falling around her face as she cradled her head in her hands.

Cloe sat cross-legged next to Saffron and laid her hand on the other girl's arm. "We can practise together," she suggested. "It'll help us both get better."

For the first time, Saffron gave her a smile, though she still looked unconvinced. "Maybe that'll help," she murmured. "Or maybe I'm just not cut out for clowning."

"Well, girls, I think it's time for a break," Marisol interrupted, looking worriedly at her devastated student. "We'll try another activity in a little bit, okay?"

Cloe tried to help Saffron up, but the girl just shook her head. "I just need a little bit of time alone," she said softly.

Grabbing her forest green jacket, Cloe walked outside, resisting the urge to do a funny walk like the ones she had tried earlier because she was afraid it would look like she was showing off in front of her classmate. She felt bad for Saffron, but she was also really happy that her instinct had been right and that she seemed to have a real talent for clowning.

CHAPTER 8

"So, who's ready to try a high-flying catch?" Anjelica asked her students.

After a few more practise swings on the high trapeze, Sasha was totally ready to try the next move, so she shot her hand into the air. "I am!"

"What, and I'm supposed to catch her?" Cadence demanded.

"No, Cadence, you aren't ready to be a catcher yet," Anjelica informed her. "It's very dangerous for an inexperienced trapeze artist to try catching another flyer. So I'll be catching each of you when you give it a try."

"Then I think I should get to go first," Cadence replied, "since I'm the more advanced student and all." She shouldered her way past Sasha to stand directly in front of their teacher.

"Go ahead," Sasha said with a shrug. "We'll both get our turns."

"That's the kind of attitude I like to see," their teacher declared approvingly. "But before anyone tries it, we need to do some prep work."

She released the low trapezes again and told the girls, "Now try hanging by your knees with your hands gripping the bar in between them."

Both girls climbed on, hanging upside down with their ponytails brushing the floor.

"Now release your hands and arch back," Anjelica continued, and the girls followed her instructions so their hands dangled toward the ground. "Those are all the moves you'll need to do the knee hang on the high trapeze for real."

Sasha and Cadence clambered off their trapezes, and Cadence climbed the ladder to the platform high above them, with Anjelica following. As their teacher held the high trapeze steady, she explained, "You'll start out just doing the normal swing, but when I say 'legs up', you'll hook your knees over the bar like you just did down there." She gestured towards the ground far below. "Ready?"

Cadence nodded and grasped the bar with both hands. "Set," Anjelica called, and Cadence bent her knees. "Hep!" With that, Cadence jumped up and began swinging.

On her backswing, Anjelica shouted to her, "Legs up!"

Cadence flipped over to loop her knees over the bar, while Sasha watched in amazement. Her classmate wasn't exactly her favorite person, but she had to admit that the girl had style. Sasha only hoped she

could manage the knee hang as smoothly when her turn came.

"Point your toes down," Anjelica reminded Cadence and then, as the girl started to swing out again, she cried, "Hands off now!" The girl released the bar, arching her back as their teacher had taught them on the low bars.

"Now, hands back up," their teacher continued, and Cadence grabbed hold of the bar once more. "And legs back down." The girl took her legs off the bar so she was hanging by her hands once more, just the way she had started out. "And release."

Cadence let go of the bar and Anjelica lowered her to the mat below.

"Excellent job!" their teacher announced. "You're right, Cadence – you're definitely ready to try the catch."

Cadence preened under the teacher's

praise, pausing only to shoot Sasha a superior glance.

"All right, Sasha, you're up!" Anjelica told her.

Sasha climbed the ladder quickly, eager

to give this new move a try. As she looked out across the room, she felt her heart beating faster, though more due to a rush of adrenaline than fear. Before she knew it, she was swinging through the air again, and it was just as much of an amazing rush as the first time she tried it. Then, following her teacher's commands, she was hanging upside down, with the world rushing past inverted. Once she was right side up again, she released the bar and sank to the floor by her safety line.

"Wow," was all Sasha could say. "This just gets better and better!"

"It sure does," Anjelica agreed. She ran the girls through the knee hang a few more times before announcing that they were truly ready to try a catch. "For this, we'll need a safety net," she added, and with the Sasha and Cadence's help, she secured the net beneath them.

She climbed the opposite platform and had both girls climb the other platform so one could hold the trapeze for the other.

"You'll do your knee hang just like before, but when you come to the end of your second swing, I'll wrap my hands around your wrists as you release the bar," Anjelica announced. "Make sense?"

The girls nodded, and Cadence wrapped her long fingers around the bar. She swung out and back, then looped her knees over the bar and swung once more before releasing her hands.

Opposite her, Anjelica was waiting, hanging from the other high trapeze by her knees, her position the reverse of Cadence's. Facing her student, Anjelica reached out her arms and, at exactly the right moment, grasped Cadence's wrists. Cadence locked her hands around Anjelica's wrists as well and slid her knees off the bar, and then she was swinging back and forth, hanging from her teacher's hands like a professional trapeze artist.

"Okay, I'm about to let go," Anjelica told Cadence before releasing her grip. Cadence bounced onto the safety net below and burst into a fit of giggles.

"That was so much fun!" she squealed.

"My turn!" Sasha exclaimed. She and Cadence climbed back up, and Sasha repeated her classmate's movements. When it was time for the catch, she grabbed her teacher's wrists, released the trapeze, and shouted, "Woohoo!" as she swung through the air before dropping onto the net.

"Okay, that was the coolest thing ever!" Sasha cried.

"Oh, there's more," Anjelica assured her. "Feel like learning a few more tricks?"

"You know it!" Sasha agreed.

"So next, let's try the splits," Anjelica continued. "Back to the low trapezes so I can show you a few more moves."

She showed them first position, where, upside down, they held one knee bent and the other straight, their toes pointed, and then had them go into the splits. "Then you'll do the catch, and this time, when I release, you'll grab back onto your own trapeze. Think you can handle it?"

"Totally!" Sasha assured her. This time, she got to go first. She swung out, hanging from the trapeze by her hands, then flipped over and put her legs in the first position, then did the splits and, as she swung out, her teacher caught her again. As she swung towards her trapeze, Anjelica let go of her hands and for a moment Sasha was flying through the air, feeling completely free. Then she spun around, grabbed the bar with both hands, and swung back onto the platform.

"Ohmigosh, I can't believe I pulled that off!" Sasha cried.

"Yeah, I can't believe it either," Cadence muttered from below. "Now, watch this," she called over her shoulder as she climbed back to the top. She did the splits and catch perfectly, but when she tried to grab her own trapeze again, she missed, flailing down towards the net, suspended by her safety wire.

"Not bad," Anjelica told her. "Why don't you try it again?"

Looking embarrassed, Cadence made her way up the ladder again, her head lowered.

"Don't lose your confidence," Anjelica called. "You'll get it this time!"

Cadence drew in a deep breath and went through the trick again – and this time she caught the trapeze on the way back.

"Yay!" Sasha cheered, clapping as loud as

she could. Even though Cadence hadn't been very supportive of her, Sasha was determined to be a good sport. And she was pretty sure she caught a grateful expression on Cadence's face as she made her way back down. Still, Sasha had to admit to herself that she didn't mind seeing the other girl brought down just a notch. Maybe Cadence wasn't quite the pro trapeze artist she thought she was just yet.

CHAPTER 9

After spending a half-day in their chosen classes, the girls all switched and tried another one. The next day, they each spent a half-day in the two classes they hadn't had yet. On the afternoon of the second day of camp, they all gathered in the school's lobby again so they could choose their specialities for the rest of the week.

"Now that you've had a chance to try everything the school has to offer, does everyone know what they want to focus on as their circus act?" Anjelica asked.

"I'd like to stick with my first choice," Yasmin said, and her three best friends all said the same.

"Would anyone like to switch?" Anjelica wanted to know.

While the other girls shook their heads, Saffron said quietly, "I would." Then, louder, she said, "I just don't think clowning is my thing, that's all."

"Okay, then, does anyone else want to take Saffron's slot in our clown course?" Anjelica looked around at each of her students, and after a moment Kylie stepped forward to volunteer.

"Sure, I'll give it a whirl." She glanced over at Saffron and added, "If you'd be cool with being a magician, that is."

"Ohmigosh, I would love to!" Saffron cried, looking totally relieved.

"Oh, good, that's settled then." Anjelica smiled at all of her students and added, "So we'll see you all back here tomorrow, and you'll start really delving into each of your arts. Have a great night!"

Cloe, Jade, Sasha and Yasmin headed for Yasmin's Corvette and drove back over to her place for a sleepover.

"My clown class is gonna be so much more fun with Kylie in it," Cloe declared.

"Was Saffron totally awful?" Sasha asked. "I mean, she made it pretty obvious that she didn't even want to do the class to begin with, so she couldn't have been much fun to clown with."

"Actually, it was kind of sad," Cloe replied. "She just had a really hard time with the whole clowning thing."

"So she wasn't funny?" Yasmin asked.

"Honestly? No," Cloe admitted.

"See, I found it totally bizarre being a clown, didn't you?" Jade sat cross-legged on Yasmin's plush floor pillows, facing her friends.

"No, it's actually awesome!" Cloe cried. "Didn't you guys love getting to invent your own characters and design cool looks for them?"

"I don't know," Jade said. "I wasn't really feeling the clown designs."

"But it's so much fun!" Cloe protested.

"Yeah, but you're the one who loves to perform," Yasmin pointed out, "so of course you'd love dreaming up a totally original character!"

"So are you guys having fun with your classes?" Cloe asked. She leaned over and

grabbed some popcorn from the bowlful that Yasmin had made and popped a handful into her mouth.

"Ohmigosh, animal training is the best!" Yasmin declared. "I love my horse, Snowflake – she totally responds to me, and I feel like I'm really getting the hang of trick riding!"

"I can't wait to see you in that ring," Sasha told her. "You're so good with animals – I'm sure you're utterly amazing!"

"Aww, thanks, Sash!" Sitting beside Sasha on the bed, Yasmin reached over and gave her best friend a hug. "And I really can't wait to see you whizzing through the air on the trapeze!"

"Isn't riding the trapeze just the coolest thing ever?" Sasha looked at her friends eagerly, and they had to laugh at the excitement on her face.

"It is pretty fun," Yasmin agreed, "but my fear of heights makes it a little less than ideal for me."

"Good point," Sasha admitted. "Well, I'm totally proud of you for facing your fear and trying it anyway!"

"So, Jade, do you know how to make our classmates disappear yet?" Cloe joked, throwing a kernel of popcorn playfully at her friend.

"Nah, but I'm hoping to learn that tomorrow," Jade told her. "Especially since now I'll have Saffron to practise on!"

"Seriously, what is up with those girls?" Yasmin wanted to know.

She flopped back on her bed, staring at the ceiling with it's star-shaped decorations.

"I think they're just really competitive." Sasha slid onto the floor and grabbed a bottle of water from Yasmin's mini-fridge. "I mean, they are totally focused on being the best."

"Yeah, well, I'm pretty competitive too," Jade pointed out, "but I don't feel the need to be totally mean about it like they do!"

"Hey, are we really gonna put on our own circus?" Cloe asked.

"I think we're all supposed to perform in the school's circus at the end of next week, right?" Yasmin sat back up so she could see her friends.

"But wouldn't it be way more fun if we did our own?" Sasha leaned forwards, excited. "Maybe we could even have a circus-off with the other girls, you know? Prove who's better, once and for all!"

Yasmin shook her head. "I really don't think Anjelica would go for that. She doesn't seem like she's really into competition."

"But that's exactly why she should let us try it," Jade insisted. "She's seen how snotty those girls are to us, so how can she expect us to perform with them?"

"Don't you think real circus performers have to go on with people they aren't totally thrilled with sometimes?" Yasmin pointed out. "If we want to act like real pros, we need to learn how to do the same."

"It'd be so cool to have our very own circus, though!" Cloe cried. "Why don't we at least ask and see what Anjelica says?"

"Okay," Yasmin agreed after a moment. "But if she doesn't like the idea, we've got to find a way to deal with those other girls, okay?"

"Of course," Sasha promised. With a laugh, she added, "But the question is, can *they* find a way to deal with *us*?"

Her friends laughed too, but Yasmin stopped suddenly. "Hey, what about Kylie? If we don't have to be stuck with those girls, she shouldn't either. She's really sweet."

"Good point," Cloe replied. "Sure, we could double up on the clowns, right?"

"Yeah, she was really good in the clown class we had together," Jade told the others. "We should totally invite her to join us."

"Sounds like a plan, ladies," Yasmin declared. "Now, who's ready for a makeover?" She grabbed her sparkly make-up kit from her bedside table and held it up to her friends.

"Me first!" Jade cried. "But no clown make-up, okay, Clo?"

Giggling, Cloe said, "Hey, no promises. But even if I give you a clown makeover, I can promise you it'll still be totally cute!"

"I'd believe that," Sasha agreed as they all began rifling through Yasmin's make-up collection, thinking up cool looks for all their best friends.

CHAPTER 10

Even though they were sleepy from their late night of talking and laughing, the girls arrived at the School of Circus Arts early the next day so they could talk to Anjelica about their plans for putting together their own circus at the end of the camp.

They found her in her office, typing rapidly on her computer, but when she looked up and saw them, she flashed them all a welcoming smile. "What's up, girls?" she asked politely.

"We actually had a question about the final performance," Sasha explained. "We were wondering if, well, if it would be okay if our class split into two groups, and put on two smaller circuses instead of doing one all together."

Anjelica looked surprised, and the girls started to get nervous. "But if you don't want us to, that's totally fine, too," Cloe told her in a rush.

"No, no, it's not that," their teacher assured them. "It's just, Cadence, Meadow and Saffron came by after camp yesterday and asked me the same thing." She looked seriously from one girl to the next. "Are you guys having some sort of feud that I should be worried about? Because in the circus arts, it's really important that you're all able to trust and depend on each other."

"Not a feud, exactly," Jade replied. "But you might have noticed that they aren't exactly our biggest fans."

"I have noticed that," Anjelica admitted, "and I have to say I don't like it. The other teachers have noticed the same thing. So when the other girls came in here to talk to me, I gave them an earful about how to be good sports. Hopefully it'll get better now."

"I really hope you're right," Yasmin said.

"So does that mean you want us to perform with them after all?" Cloe asked.

Anjelica sighed, and shook her head. "No. After I gave the girls my speech, they said they didn't want to finish the camp if they couldn't put on their own show. They said the whole reason they're doing this programme is so they can master their three-girl act, and if they don't get to do that, there's no point to them being here."

"That's awful!" Sasha cried. "I mean, they aren't my favourite people either, but I wouldn't give up learning from you teachers for anything!"

"Now that's what I like to hear!" Anjelica exclaimed. "But anyway, yes, you girls can have your own show. And I'm sure it'll be amazing, judging from your efforts so far."

"Oh yeah, we'll totally make you proud!" Cloe promised.

"I know you will," Anjelica agreed. She stood up and walked around her desk, beaming at the girls. "I'm so glad you all joined my school, you know."

The girls left her office and strolled into the courtyard in front of the school with huge smiles on their faces.

"So, should we start rehearsing tonight?" Sasha suggested. Her friends burst into laughter – Sasha was totally organized, so she was always the one who insisted that they practise as much as possible for whatever their latest performance was.

"You know, I think I'll be kind of magicked out after eight hours straight of practising," Jade pointed out. "Maybe we should wait till this weekend when we *don't* have classes to start putting our circus together. What do you think?"

"Makes sense to me," Yasmin agreed.

"Yeah, but don't you think those other girls are prepping for their show already?" Cloe asked, worriedly.

"So what if they are?" Jade told her. "They can waste their energy on that if they want, but in the meantime, we'll be perfecting our individual arts, and *then* we'll whip up an awesome circus all of our own."

"I like the way you think," Yasmin declared, slinging her arm around her best friend's shoulders.

Just then, Kylie strolled up with a friendly smile on her face. "Hey, girls, what's up?"

"Oh, Kylie, we actually wanted to talk to you," Sasha said. "We're forming our own circus, and we wanted to invite you to join."

The smile faded from Kylie's face, and she wouldn't meet the other girls' eyes.

"Kylie, what's wrong?" Yasmin asked worriedly, touching her friend's arm reassuringly.

"Oh, it's just ... well, um, I don't know how to say this," Kylie stammered. "But, see, Cadence, Meadow and Saffron asked me to join their circus. And ... I said yes."

"Why would you do that?" Jade cried. "They're totally mean!"

"Well, yeah, I know, but ... I mean, they have been a lot nicer to me lately, so, well, I thought I'd give them a chance." Kylie stared at her feet, clearly miserable.

"It's fine by us," Sasha assured her. "It's just that we want to make sure you're okay with performing with them."

"Oh, I am!" Kylie insisted. "And, you know, those girls go to my school, and I'm hoping, well ..." She hung her head again, too embarrassed to say anything more.

"You're hoping they'll be nicer to you at school if you do a good job with them in this circus," Yasmin finished for her, and Kylie nodded slowly.

"Hey, we totally understand, and I hope you're right," Jade told her. "But if they aren't nice to you, you can always come and join us."

"Aww, thanks," Kylie said, looking touched. "You girls are just so sweet!" Then she glanced at her watch and gasped. "Oh no, we have a Circus Sparkle meeting right now – I'd better run!" She hurried off, waving at the other girls over her shoulder.

"I can't believe she agreed to perform with them," Cloe murmured once Kylie was out of earshot. "They're totally mean to her!"

"I can't believe they asked her!" Jade added, clearly frustrated.

"Well, maybe they will start treating her better after this so it will be worth it for her," Yasmin suggested hopefully.

"Yeah, as long as she doesn't make a single mistake," Sasha pointed out. "If she does, she'd better watch out – those girls will be all over her!"

"But everyone makes mistakes! No one is perfect!" Cloe cried.

"Exactly," Sasha agreed. "But hey, it's her choice, and hopefully it'll all work out okay for them all."

"Okay, girls, time to go and soak up lots of circus know-how so we can have the awesomest circus in town!" Yasmin declared.

After a quick group hug, each girl headed to her own class with the knowledge that all of their classmates were now their competition — which wasn't exactly a comforting feeling.

CHAPTER 11

"I am a trapeze master!" Sasha declared that weekend, making her friends giggle. "Seriously, wait till you see all the amazing new tricks I've learned!"

She and her friends were strolling down their town's main street on their way to dinner at one of their favourite restaurants, Carousel. After a week of intense training at their camp, they figured they deserved a little celebration to let off steam.

"Well, I am a totally dazzling magician, if I do say so myself," Jade chimed in.

"And I am an unstoppable animal trainer!" Yasmin added. "Today I even got to train an elephant. How cool is that?"

"Pretty cool," Cloe agreed. "*Almost* as cool as my unbelievable clowning skills!"

"I am so excited to see all of you girls showing off your new talents!" Yasmin led the way into the restaurant and up to the hostess stand. "Yasmin, party of four," she told the hostess.

"Of course," the hostess said politely. "Right this way." She led the girls to their favourite table, next to the windows but with a clear view of the gorgeous antique carousel that the restaurant was named for in the atrium at the centre of the room. "Enjoy your meal." After passing out their menus, the hostess pivoted on her platform heel and strutted away.

"Ooh, I love this place," Cloe sighed as she settled into her chair.

"I know!" Jade cried. "I mean, what other restaurant do you know that has its very own carousel? It's so chic."

"Do you know the story of this place?" Yasmin asked.

"Yas, you give us the full history every time we come here!" Sasha protested. "We know this building used to be an indoor entertainment gallery, with games and souvenir shops and all that."

"And when that closed down, the chef here bought the building, turned it into a fabulous restaurant, and even restored the carousel," Jade chimed in.

"And it's been our favourite restaurant ever since!" Cloe added.

"Okay, okay, I guess you girls *have* been listening!" Yasmin peered at her friends over her menu, smiling. "So, what sounds good tonight?"

"Mmm, it all does!" Cloe cried, scanning the menu. "Can we order one of everything?"

"Yeah, but I might have some trouble doing my high-flying flips if I eat the entire menu!" Sasha pointed out.

"All right, if you insist," Cloe sighed. "I guess I can manage to choose just one entrée, if I have to."

After they placed their orders, the girls turned their attention to the major issue at hand – their upcoming circus performance.

"We'll time to rehearse all week at camp, right?" Jade asked.

"Yeah, but if we're gonna edge out those other girls, we need to get in all the practise we can," Sasha pointed out.

"Except I can't practise without the school's animals," Yasmin reminded her, "and Sasha, I doubt you can manage the trapeze without, you know, the trapeze."

"Don't you think Anjelica will let us get in some extra hours of rehearsal time?" Yasmin asked.

"Maybe," Sasha replied. "But she has a lot of regular students to squeeze in on the weekend, since our camp's hogging the facilities all week right now."

"Plus the Circus Sparkle girls have probably already snagged whatever extra time they might have," Cloe added. "They seem to always manage to keep a step ahead of us somehow."

"Speaking of which – they already have a cute name for their circus, and we still need one," Jade pointed out. "Any ideas? Come on Yas, work your creative magic!"

Gazing at the vibrantly coloured carousel with its hand-sculpted horses, Yasmin suggested, "What about calling it the Carousel Circus?"

"Yas, that's totally adorable!" Sasha declared. "We can always count on you to dream up a fabulous name for our latest enterprise Pretty Princess."

"Hey, that's what I do," Yasmin replied with a modest shrug.

"And that's why we love you!" Cloe exclaimed. "Well – one of the many reasons."

"Okay, so we've got the name – now, how do we want our show to go?" Sasha asked.

"I thought we could open with me working the crowd," Cloe suggested. Her friends exchanged smiles – Cloe was always eager to take centre stage. "No, seriously – I've learned some fun ways to warm up the audience that I think will really get our show off to an awesome start."

"I like it," Jade chimed it. "Jokes are always a great opener. And from there, maybe we could go into my magic act."

"And then I'll bring out the horses, and Sasha's trapeze act will be the grand finale!" Yasmin cried.

"That'll be such a spectacular show!" Cloe squealed with delight.

"Hey, our shows always are," Sasha replied with a smile.

"But wait, Sasha, how are you going to manage the trapeze all by yourself?" Yasmin asked with a quizzical look on her face.

"Oh, Anjelica is going to help out with both circuses," Sasha explained. "The trapeze really doesn't work with just one person, or at least not safely!"

"Ooh, I wonder if I can get Isabelle to join me in the ring, too," Yasmin replied. "Circus horse routines look so much cooler when there are two horses moving in synch."

"I'm sure she would help you out," Jade told her. "She seems super-sweet."

"Do you think I should ask Marisol to be in our show too?" Cloe wondered. "I don't want her to feel insulted if I don't ask her … but it's just that I want to do as much of this on our own as possible!"

"Can't you guys work up some fun tandem routines, though?" Jade enquired, and Cloe nodded. "I'm thinking of seeing if Marlin will be my magician's assistant. I mean, The Amazing Jade needs an assistant, right?"

"I'm sure the Circus Sparkle girls are including our teachers in all of their routines," Sasha added. "So why shouldn't we make full use of their talents, too?"

"True," Cloe admitted. "But do you think it's fair to make them perform in both circuses? I mean, that sounds pretty exhausting!"

"Yeah, but they're pros," Jade pointed out. "I think they can handle doing two shows in one night."

"That's true," Yasmin agreed. "The Sterling

Sisters Circus does double-headers all the time, and they were the star performers for that circus, so you know they were in the ring for every show!"

"I can't think of a better way to ring in the New Year than in the middle of our own circus big top!" Cloe added. She thought it was totally cool that their camp's finale was being held on New Year's Eve, right before the end of winter break.

"Let's swing by the school tomorrow and ask them all to help us out," Sasha suggested. "Then we'll be all set to finalize our routines." Their waitress set their food in front of them, and Sasha added, "And in the meantime, why don't we just relax and enjoy our meal?"

"Wait, Sasha thinks we should relax, instead of rehearsing 24/7?" Jade teased. "What is the world coming to?"

"I know, it's weird!" Sasha admitted. "But

really, I think spending all day, every day working on our routines will be plenty!"

Grinning, the girls dug into their meals, talking happily about their plans for their new circus.

CHAPTER 12

The girls had never worked harder in their lives. They spent all day at camp, snatched a few extra hours with their instructors whenever they could, and by the time their big New Year's Eve finale show rolled around, they had their routines totally down and perfected.

Under Jade's direction, the girls had made their own costumes. For Cloe, the pretty pink dress she had drawn, along with all the accessories. Jade made herself a white blouse with a black bow, a denim corset, jeans, and high-heeled Mary Jane shoes. Once she tried on her costume, she felt like a real magician, but with her own sense of fashion flair!

Sasha put together a short ruffled red and yellow skirt paired with black bicycle shorts, and a red and white striped top with balloon sleeves. She wore high heels too, although she planned to change into ballet slippers for her actual performance.

Finally, Yasmin looked sleek and sophisticated in her riding gear – a black and white fitted jacked with wide fuchsia lapels over a black cami, skinny fit black pants with a hot-pink contrast stripe down the front, topped off with her hair tucked into a bun and a little top hat atop her head.

"Well, no matter how the show goes, we'll definitely be the cutest performers in the ring," Jade declared once they were all decked out in their new gear.

"Oh, we'll be the best ones, too!" Sasha chimed in.

"Yeah!" her friends all cheered, giving each other high fives.

They drove over to the School of Circus Arts, where they were slated for one last dress rehearsal before their big show.

But when they arrived, they discovered that, once more, their rivals had beaten them to it.

"Um, is that really what you're wearing?" Cadence asked as soon as she spotted the girls. She and her friends were dressed in matching red sparkly circus leotards. "Not exactly a unified look, is it?"

"Well, we like to use our clothes to express ourselves," Jade replied. "And we think it totally works!"

"Well, you go ahead and keep thinking that," Meadow scoffed. Standing behind her, Kylie looked upset at this dig, but didn't say a word.

"Look, girls, this whole competition thing has been fun," Sasha interrupted, "but don't you think it's enough already? I mean, we're all here to have fun, right?"

"Maybe it's just fun and games to *you*,"

Saffron snapped, "but we're planning on becoming circus performers for real, so we take this way seriously."

"You know, taking it seriously doesn't mean you have to be rude," Jade pointed out.

"Ladies, what's going on here?" Anjelica strolled up with her fellow teachers following behind. The teachers were all dressed in neutral black costumes that would fit in with both circuses' looks.

"Just a little friendly competition," Cadence replied.

"Well, just see that it stays friendly," Anjelica told her, sounding suspicious. "But for now, let's get you girls into the ring. We only have a few hours till show time!"

Circus Sparkle went first, while the Carousel Circus girls watched from the stands in the school's central arena. Like their circus, this one began with their clown, Kylie, doing a routine with Marisol.

Throughout her act, Kylie seemed unsure of herself, her motions stiff, her smile forced. "Okay, Kylie, can we try that again?" Meadow asked at the end of the routine. "Except this time, could we make it, you know, *funny*?"

Kylie looked crushed, and Marisol told her, "I think that was a very good effort for a beginner."

"Well, I'm sorry, but we don't need a good effort right now!" Cadence snapped. "We're about to make our professional debut, so we need all of our acts to be better than a good effort right now."

"You can do it, Kylie!" Cloe shouted from the audience,

pumping her arm encouragingly in the air. Kylie shot her a weak smile, but she looked even more uncomfortable as she ran through her act again.

"We need to do that again," Saffron announced, but Anjelica shook her head.

"Actually, we need to move on," their teacher informed them. "We have to get through the rest of your performances and then, if you'll recall, there's another circus that needs to rehearse as well."

"Fine!" Meadow stomped to the side of the ring, where she grabbed her horse, Moonlight, and swung onto his back. The horse, sensing her frustration, was jittery, and shied away from her commands.

Isabelle followed her into the ring on Snowflake, and reminded Meadow, "Horses can sense your feelings. If you don't calm down, Moonlight will be too on edge to do anything you want him to."

"I've been riding since I was five," Meadow snapped, "and I've never had any trouble getting a horse to do what I want. I'm certainly not going to let Moonlight be the first one to outsmart me."

"Moonlight *is* a very smart horse," Yasmin murmured to her friends in the stands. "I bet he could teach her a thing or two given half-a-chance!"

"No doubt," Jade whispered back.

Meadow's whole act was off, and the more things that went wrong, the more furious she got which, of course, only agitated her horse even more. "There's seriously something wrong with this horse!" she shouted. "I need a new one for the show, or this is never going to work!"

"It's not the horse, it's the rider," Isabelle explained. "I can switch horses with you if you want, but I can promise you that Snowflake will react to you in exactly the same way."

"Meadow, why don't you take a breather?" Anjelica suggested. "We can come back to you once you've had a chance to cool off."

"Whatever!" Meadow slid off of her horse's back and dropped the reins, not even bothering to lead him back to the holding pen offstage. She just stalked over to her friends, and they all leaned their heads together, whispering furiously, while poor Kylie stood alone, looking dejected.

Next up was Saffron, but her magic tricks kept falling flat. "See, magic is all about your flow – if you aren't in the zone, there's no way you'll convince the audience that anything you're doing is real," Jade murmured to her friends.

"She's definitely not in the zone," Yasmin agreed. "Not anywhere near!"

"Let me try that again!" Saffron cried, scurrying after Magic the Bunny, who had

hopped out of her hat in the middle of her trick. With Marlin's help, she caught the rabbit and started her routine over again.

"This is a disaster!" Cadence cried. "Luckily, I'm here to save the day!" She climbed up the ladder to the trapeze platform, while Anjelica did the same on the ladder opposite her. Cadence took hold of the bar, and launched herself off, doing a few flips in the air before her teacher caught her. Just as quickly, Anjelica released her again, and Cadence grabbed the trapeze once more, then swung back, did the splits, and grasped her teacher's wrists again.

But when her teacher let go this time, Cadence swung back, reached for the bar — and totally missed. As she dropped to the safety net below, Cadence wailed, "Nooo!"

"Ohmigosh, are you okay?" Sasha gasped, rushing over to check on her classmate.

"I'm fine," Cadence informed her, stumbling her way out of the net. "It's just my circus that's completely falling apart."

"*Your* circus?" Saffron cried. "I'm sorry, but I thought this was *our* circus."

"Yeah, well, you're the one who couldn't even handle the *clown* class," Cadence snapped. "And that's gotta be the easiest class here!"

"Are you kidding me?" Saffron demanded. "Clowning is *hard*."

"And apparently magic is really hard for you, too," Cadence continued.

"Ooh, that is *it*!" Saffron declared. "I'm so out of here!"

"Fine!" Cadence shouted after her, as her friend stalked off. "You weren't exactly pulling your weight, anyway!"

"You know what?" Meadow asked. "If Saffron goes, I go. I don't need this, anyway." With that, she followed her friend out of the circus arena.

"Well, I'm not staying here with *her*," Cadence scoffed, pointing towards Kylie. "So I guess that Circus Sparkle is officially out." She stomped out of the ring after the others without a backward glance.

Kylie looked like she was close to tears, so Cloe, Jade, Sasha and Yasmin hurried over to comfort her. "My mess-up made everyone else mess up," she sniffled. "This is totally my fault you guys!"

"No way!" Jade protested. "Those girls were a meltdown waiting to happen."

"I just really wanted to be in a circus," Kylie sighed. "It looks like so much fun!"

"Then be in our circus," Yasmin begged.

"Really?" Kylie gasped, her eyes wide as she looked from one girl to the next.

"Totally!" Jade squealed. "Would you mind being my magician's assistant?"

"I would love to," Kylie agreed. "I liked magic best anyway, but I thought it would make those girls happy if I switched. And since I haven't had that much practise, it would be super if you could take the lead."

Jade turned to her magic teacher and asked, "You know what I bet you would be fantastic at? Being our ringmaster!"

"Actually, I've always wanted to try my hand at that," Marlin told them. "I'd be happy to step up!"

"Wait, what is Kylie gonna wear?" Sasha gasped. "She's gotta look super-stylin'!"

"Don't you still have that circus-inspired outfit you wore a couple of weeks ago?" Yasmin asked. "That would be totally cute magician's assistant gear."

"Ooh, you're right!" Sasha agreed. "It's in my closet at home – I'll go and get it and be back in a flash!" While Sasha hurried home, her friends and their teachers hurried to revamp their show, expanding their acts since they would be the only show of the night, and adding in banter from Marlin, who proved to be a truly talented ringmaster.

Sasha rushed back into the arena, and Kylie slipped backstage to change. When she emerged, the girls were all amazed at her daring new look. "I think that looks better on you than it did on me," Sasha declared. "You might just have to keep it!"

Kylie blushed, but did a little twirl as her new friends applauded. Jade and Kylie practised their new act, and then suddenly, the audience began filing in, so the girls all scurried backstage.

"Ladies and gentleman, boys and girls, the Stilesville School of Circus Arts proudly presents the world premiere of the one, the only, Carousel Circus!" Marlin announced, and the crowd cheered wildly as Cloe and Marisol bumbled out, joking and tumbling as they wove through the stands. Within moments, waves of laughter coursed through the entire arena.

Next, Jade and Kylie made their entrance, and with a flourish, Jade made herself appear to levitate, pulled Marlin's rabbit out of her hat, and even made it look like she had sawed Kylie in half. The audience oohed and aahed in amazement, clapping like crazy as the magicians headed out of the ring.

Then Yasmin and Isabelle rode out in perfect tandem, standing up in their saddles, riding backward, and finishing by leaping across to land atop each other's horses. Once more, the crowd seemed overcome with excitement.

Finally, the spotlight came up on Sasha on one trapeze platform, and Anjelica on the other. "And here they are, our trapeze stars, The Amazing Anjelica and Sizzlin' Sasha!" Marlin shouted.

Sasha began swinging, flipping, spinning and twisting mid-air, just like the Soaring Santinis she had seen for the first time only a few weeks ago. For their grand finale, Sasha

and Anjelica both somersaulted off of their trapezes, flying past each other in the air above the ring, and ending up on the opposite trapeze, both smiling wildly.

The crowd went wild as Sasha and Anjelica stood up on their trapezes, waving to the audience, before returning to the two high platforms to come back down to earth.

The girls and their teachers all met in the centre of the ring, where they took a bow to a standing ovation.

"Thank you, thank you," Marlin said. "But now, it's time for our countdown to midnight, so please join us in ringing in the New Year!"

"Ten, nine, eight, seven, six, five, four, three, two, one!" The audience shouted in unison, and at one, a net full of balloons and confetti dropped from the ceiling, drifting down over all of them.

"Happy New Year!" Cloe, Jade, Sasha

and Yasmin exclaimed to each other, jumping up and down in a group hug. Kylie hung back, but they pulled her into their hug too.

"I can't think of a better way to welcome a new year than by bringing down the house with my best friends," Yasmin declared.

"And don't forget – when we go back to school, we have a new adventure to take on – starring in the school play together!" Sasha added.

"You know, now that we're big circus stars, I'm sure starring in *Under*

the Big Top will be a breeze," Cloe told her friends with a huge smile.

"Okay, but for now, let's enjoy our fans' appreciation," Jade suggested. They all turned to face the audience again, smiling and bowing as the crowd cheered and cheered.

"You know," Sasha said as she gathered up bouquets of roses that their fans tossed into the ring, "I could totally get used to this level of adoration!"

"Well, you'd better," Anjelica told her. "Because the Carousel Circus is a huge hit, and I think you girls should be prepared to go on tour!"

The girls looked at each other, grinning, and Jade exclaimed, "You know I love a tour girls, any excuse to spend time with you."

"Me too!" the girls all chorused before taking a final bow and rushing offstage to celebrate an exciting start to the new year alongside their very best friends.

Read more about Bratz in these other awesome books!

Control your own Bratz™ Stories on DVD!

• Loads of different story line combinations
• Music Videos • Fun Activities and more!

CONTROL YOUR OWN BRATZ™ STORIES

Livin' IT UP WITH THE BRATZ

BRATZ GLITZ 'N' GLAMOUR

ALL NEW! You take control 8 story lines Fun Activities and more

BRATZ REALLY Girlz Rock Coming Soon To DVD

For more information & to be kept up to date with new exciting Bratz™ DVD releases just email to bratz@lionsgatefilms.co.uk

OUT NOW!

LIONSGATE

TM & © MGA Entertainment, Inc. BRATZ™, BRATZ KIDZ™ and all related logos, names, characters, distinctive likenesses and slogans are the exclusive property of MGA. All rights reserved. Used under license by XLT. © Lions Gate Home Entertainment UK Ltd. All Rights Reserved.